WILL MAN FLY?

And Other Strange & Wonderful Predictions from the 1890s

compiled by
Dave Walter

American & World Geographic Publishing

ISBN 1-56037-027-0
Compilation and Introduction © 1993 Dave Walter,
excerpted from his book Today Then
from the same publisher.
© 1993 American & World Geographic Publishing
All rights reserved.

Printed in U.S.A.

Contents

Introduction 4
Medicine 8
Religion & Theology 11
Relationship of Capital & Labor 14
Accumulation of Wealth 17
Criminal Justice 20
Education 23
The Servant Problem 27
Fashionable Dress 29
Temperance Legislation 32
Postal Service 35
Transportation 38
Railroad/Telegraph Ownership 50
Federal Government 54
The State of the Arts 62
The South & the West 68
Monetary System 71
The Legal Profession 73
Divorce 75
Agriculture 77
Status of Women 81
American Indians 85
Architecture 88
Technology 90
Greatest City in America 98
Most-Honored American 104
Happier, Healthier, Handsomer 107
The United States in the 1990s 113
The World in the 1990s 120
Last Words 127

Introduction

Will Man Fly? presents selections from 74 pieces written in the early 1890s by noted commentators on the American scene. The American Press Association, a ready-print syndicate based in New York City, originally commissioned the writings. The A.P.A. ran this series in weekly newspapers across the country as a prelude to the opening of the World's Columbian Exposition in Chicago on May 1, 1893. The complete essays from which these excerpts come are reproduced in my book *Today Then*.

The writers were asked to predict aspects of American society 100 years hence—in the 1990s. In the process, they produce insights into American life *both* in the 1890s and in the 1990s.

The United States of the early 1890s exhibited all of the strengths, all of the promises, and all of the problems of a young nation. It had bumped and stumbled through childhood and adolescence. With no little luck, it emerged in the last decade of the Nineteenth Century a virile, exuberant country of immense potential—but a nation caught in paradox.

Certainly the U.S. remained in the shadow of its European parents in international relations and the arts. Yet it had settled North America from the Atlantic to the Pacific, and it was beginning to look both north and south.

Manifest Destiny was proving a difficult mistress to deny, once fully embraced.

On a map, the United States of the early 1890s appears well-formed. The current Union was short only six states: Utah (1896); Oklahoma (1907); New Mexico (1912); Arizona (1912); Alaska (1959); Hawaii (1959).

American *progress* might have been divinely ordained, but it also was fraught with risk. America might have been on an expansive building spree, but it also failed to offer opportunity for all of its citizens. And all of these social strengths and weaknesses became evident in that era's greatest show: the World's Columbian Exposition, held in Chicago in 1893.

World's Fair organizers—with Congressional backing—commemorated the four-hundredth anniversary of the landing of Christopher Columbus in the Western Hemisphere with the public dedication of the fair park in Chicago. The World's Columbian Exposition played to more than 27 million fairgoers during a six-month period—and touched the lives of practically every American. It became the most famous fair ever conducted on American soil.

Given the era, the Exposition's theme was obvious: the national progress of the United States. Yet this world's fair would do more than just document the present and provide working models of the future. It would demonstrate the unity of America and hint that further progress and development would result in an eventual utopian condition.

Although the fabulous Columbian Exposition only ran for six months after its opening on the first of May, 1893, the fair left a lasting imprint on the American cultural landscape. First, the event documented the fact that the Nineteenth Century was the greatest era of civilized progress in the history of the world. Second, it offered tangible examples of what technological progress would bring to American society—from the 260-foot-high Ferris wheel to a cylinder phonograph to carbonated soft drinks.

Once Congress had chosen Chicago over New York, Washington, and St. Louis as the site of the World's Columbian Exposition, the editorial staff in the American Press Association office spawned a plan. They proposed a feature series that would benefit from the widespread interest in the Chicago extravaganza. As finally implemented, this plan provided 74 experts a platform from which to discuss aspects of American society a century hence. As conceived, each writer would be contributing to a "Chapter of Forecasts" focusing on the 1990s.

The syndicate packaged these essays in 11 weekly segments—each containing from 4 to 8 individual pieces. The segments ran in hundreds of the country's weeklies and in the Sunday feature section of scores of big-city dailies, beginning during the first week of March 1893 and concluding during the second week of May.

Thus the A.P.A. series drew hundreds of thousands of readers right into the World's Columbian Exposition. For the fair had opened on May 1, when President Grover Cleveland pressed a button in Washington, D.C., and machinery on the Exposition grounds roared into motion. Readers who had devoured the entire series were well-prepared for the startling features of the fair. In effect they had enrolled in a survey course on American social history—past, present, and future.

Technology is the ultimate culprit in skewing most of these predictions that were wrong. Few forecasters could divine the key invention (for example the automobile, or the atomic bomb, or the transistor) that would revolutionize American life 50 or 100 years hence. The futurist who can see such a key piece of technology, and can place it in a social context, becomes the true seer.

As with futurists closing the Twentieth Century, the 1890s A.P.A. writers frequently fell victim to two beliefs: that technology could and would solve society's problems; and that human nature would change dramatically for the better. It is precisely these two beliefs that render some of the 1890s predictions the most outlandish. For technology is restricted by the laws of nature, as well as by socio-economic demands, and human nature is prone to change very little, if at all.

What will be the state of medicine in the 1990s?

Longevity will be so improved that 150 years will be no unusual age to reach.

THOMAS DE WITT TALMAGE, THEOLOGIAN

Cancer and consumption will be as easily cured as influenza or a "run around" [diarrhea].

THOMAS DE WITT TALMAGE, THEOLOGIAN

The principles of medicine will be more generally and intelligently understood. There will be much more dependence on nature than on drugs or physicians, who will have decreased in number.

JUNIUS HENRI BROWNE, JOURNALIST

The occult sixth sense will be the predominant element in medicine and theology. Mesmerism will take the place of anesthetics in surgery.

ELLA WHEELER WILCOX, POET

Doctors will prescribe no more than one-third of the drugs they now think necessary.

EDWIN CHECKLEY, PHYSICAL CULTURIST

In medicine the true relation of the muscular system to the organic system—and their combined influence on the nervous system—will become more fully and generally understood. The fused action of the patient's mind and muscles will be depended on by the physician instead of drugs to prevent, allay, and cure disease.

EDWIN CHECKLEY, PHYSICAL CULTURIST

Medicine will attain the dignity of a science, having passed through the period of preliminary experiment.

THOMAS DIXON, JR., MINISTER/CINEMATOGRAPHER

What will be the state of religion/theology in the 1990s?

There will be far more religion than now. The technicalities of religion will mean nothing, and the spirit of religion will dominate. The minister's war hatchet will be buried beside Modoc's tomahawk.

THOMAS DE WITT TALMAGE, THEOLOGIAN

Theosophy—the religion of high thinking and selfless living—will take the place of creeds and dogmas. Clairvoyance or spiritual insight will be almost universal.

ELLA WHEELER WILCOX, POET

There is going to be a change in the methods of public and private benevolence. Free and indiscriminate charity will be almost unknown. Even now it is beginning to be understood that the highest charity is that which guides rather than supports. Men and women will be taught to help themselves. The aid will be given in an almost concealed manner. Self-respect will be cultivated and self-reliance as well.

DAVID H. GREER, EPISCOPAL BISHOP

All theology will be conceded to be mythology.

VAN BUREN DENSLOW, ECONOMIC ANALYST

Men and women will no longer read the Bible mechanically. On the contrary, it will be understood that it is a book to be studied. It will no longer be esteemed as gold coin, but as ore,

from which glorious and golden truths
are to be extracted.

DAVID H. GREER, EPISCOPAL BISHOP

One hundred years from now,
theology will give place to Christian
practice, and each man's faith will be
judged by his life instead of his talk.

JOHN HABBERTON, EDITOR/AUTHOR

Man will have learned the lesson
of trusting his brother. And the nation
which has drawn all peoples to it with
a cosmic gravitation and lifted them
with freedom and confidence will also
have destroyed the prejudice of race
and the animosities of sect.

ANDREW C. WHEELER (NYM CRINKLE), ART CRITIC

What will be the condition and relationship of capital and labor in the 1990s?

The condition of capital versus labor will be one of peace, with the Golden Rule prevailing.

THOMAS DE WITT TALMAGE, THEOLOGIAN

The laboring classes will always be oppressed. And the more their wages are increased, the more fatigued they will feel. I speak from experience.

BILL NYE, HUMORIST

I only hope that the brain worker will be as well paid as will be the manual laborer.

KATE FIELD, JOURNALIST/CRUSADER

Three hours will constitute a long day's work by the end of the next century. And this work will liberally furnish infinitely more of the benefits of civilization and the comforts of life than 16 hours' slavish toil will today.

MARY E. LEASE, REFORMER

───────────

The time of daily toil will be shortened to four or five hours. All willing hands will be employed, and effort will be ease.

W. A. PEFFER, KANSAS POLITICIAN

───────────

By the end of the next century, great corporations and business interests will be conducted harmoniously— on the principle of the employees and workers sharing in the profits.

JUNIUS HENRI BROWNE, JOURNALIST

The laboring classes will doubtless become thoroughly organized, and thereby attain a position of more independence as a body. The so-called laboring classes of today, when properly organized in the future, will compose the great bulk of the conservative wealth. They will produce population and will doubtless be so regulated by the laws of union as to eliminate worthless characters.

When this is attained, the entire union of the laboring class will compose a certain middle class. The third social class will be composed principally of those who are unfitted by moral habits from entering the labor ranks.

HEMPSTEAD WASHBURNE, POLITICIAN

Will the tendency toward the accumulation of wealth in the hands of a few increase or diminish by the 1990s?

A social revolution is certain to be accomplished within less than 50 years, and that will end the accumulation of wealth in the hands of the few.

THOMAS DIXON, JR., MINISTER/CINEMATOGRAPHER

The tendency toward the accumulation of great wealth in the hands of a few will decrease in the next century. The quickened conscience and the aroused conceptions of justice of an intelligent people will class the hoarder with the criminal who holds more of the world's gifts than he can possibly use, while his fellow beings want.

MARY E. LEASE, REFORMER

———————

I think that we will require the bulk of the rich man's money (when he is done with it, of course) to build national parks—and in other ways to help the nation which helped him to get hold of that money.

JOAQUIN MILLER, POET/AUTHOR

———————

The accumulation of wealth will increase in the hands of individuals, until some point in the next century. Then laws will be enacted to regulate the amount of wealth which may be inherited, so as to prevent creation of a moneyed aristocracy by inheritance.

HEMPSTEAD WASHBURNE, POLITICIAN

Already there are signs that the purpose of wealth is a divine purpose. By the end of the coming century, all wealth (to escape reproach, if for no higher reason) shall enlist itself in the volunteer service of civilization. Then the products of labor, the fruits of genius, the dividends of investment, and the spoils of commerce shall be willingly put aside in trust funds, for the ultimate use of the community.

J. P. DOLLIVER, POLITICIAN

What will be the methods used to treat criminals in the 1990s?

Changed conditions will compel the government more carefully to guard the weak from the aggressions of the strong in our society.

WILLIAM JENNINGS BRYAN, POLITICIAN

Prisons will have ventilation, and sunlight, and bathrooms, and libraries, and Christian influences that will be reformatory instead of damnatory.

THOMAS DE WITT TALMAGE, THEOLOGIAN

Criminals will be prevented from propagating their kind. This will take the place of capital punishment. And, after a few generations, this will do

away with crime, because no criminals
will be born.

ELLA WHEELER WILCOX, POET

The punishment of criminals, it
seems to me, will be based more and
more upon the effort to reform rather
than to inflict penalty. Capital punishment will be abolished. It has now
already collapsed. The only remedy
seems to be to substitute life imprison-
ment and to make the execution of law
a practical certainty upon the guilty.

THOMAS DIXON, JR., MINISTER/CINEMATOGRAPHER

By the end of the next century,
improved methods of treatment for the
confinement and punishment of crimi-

nals will be inaugurated. Much more attention will be given to their reformation than to their punishment.

SIDNEY G. BROCK, POLITICIAN/AUTHOR

Persons who chance to witness a crime will not conceal and hush it up through fear of being put in jail as witnesses, while the culprit goes free on bail.

ELIZABETH AKERS ALLEN, POET

Brutal crime will have disappeared. Subtler evils will be met by brotherly compassion, not by vindictive penalty. Ah, me. But I am thinking of a state much further in the future than the America of the 1990s.

ANNIE BESANT, REFORMER

What will be the state of common educational methods in the 1990s?

The economic and social questions of the day will be taught in the public schools. There will be no uneducated persons to act as drags on the car of progress.

T. V. POWDERLY, POPULIST EDITOR

The stuffing machine that we call the school system, which is making the rising generation a race of invalids, will be substituted by something more reasonable. No more will we have school girls with spectacles at 14, their eyes having been extinguished by overstudy, with overwrought brain. And no more will we have school boys in their dying dream trying to recite something in higher mathematics.

THOMAS DE WITT TALMAGE, THEOLOGIAN

The government will not take the child at the cradle and rear him under public supervision and under official control at the expense of the community. Rather, a wiser generation will interfere even less with him and his occupations than now.

MICHAEL D. HARTER, OHIO POLITICIAN

Educational methods will go on toward perfection in the Twentieth Century. Finally the pupil will not have to apply himself at all! But the teacher's work will grow more and more laborious.

BILL NYE, HUMORIST

The veto power that teachers now exercise over children leaving the room during school hours will be taken from them. School children will have a playground instead of a yard for recreative purposes. And they will not be made to walk around it in lockstep manner. They will rather be incited to romp, shout, and play.

EDWIN CHECKLEY, PHYSICAL CULTURIST

———————

Our public schools will train not only the mind of the pupil, but also the hand. Each child will be instructed in the manual of tools.

T. V. POWDERLY, POPULIST EDITOR

———————

The encyclopedic man, who makes a show of knowing all things, will give way to the specialist, who makes an effort to know one thing and know it well.

Education is certain to be broader and fuller. We must educate the whole man—the head, the hand, the heart. Especially must our methods be revolutionized.

Thomas Dixon, Jr.,
minister/cinematographer

What will be the future of the servant problem?

The government will establish colleges for the training of servants. Better instructed, better paid, better cared for, and more plentiful, the servant of the next century will be more useful, better content, and more respectful and respected.

ELLA WHEELER WILCOX, POET

The future of the servant problem is the same as the future of the ungodly—viz., hell.

BILL NYE, HUMORIST

Domestic life and avocations will be rendered easier, less costly, and less complex by the distribution of light, heat, and energy through storage cells or from central electric stations. Thus the "servant problem" will cease to disturb.

JOHN J. INGALLS, KANSAS POLITICIAN

For servants you will simply touch the button, and they will be turned on or off at pleasure, like water or gas by the general office.

VAN BUREN DENSLOW, ECONOMIC ANALYST

What will be the future of fashionable dress in the Twentieth Century?

Man wears too much cloth, and that cloth is cut up into too many shapes. Today man wears an average of 20 buttons each. Soon 5 buttons will be made to answer every purpose. And 100 years from now, the number will be reduced to two or three pieces of fishline.

CHARLES B. LEWIS (M. QUAD), HUMORIST

Man is bound to return to the simplicity of Biblical days. Sandals, a toga, and a cheap straw hat will replace the costumes now worn.

CHARLES B. LEWIS (M. QUAD), HUMORIST

To the degree that women own the property, they will dress plainly. The era of color in dress among women for three centuries past has been due to the fact that men held the purse. The dress of women simply certified male generosity. As women come to hold the purse and the estates, they will dress themselves more plainly. Men then will put on color and wear tights to please women.

VAN BUREN DENSLOW, ECONOMIC ANALYST

Dress, by the end of the next century, must conform more to common sense and less to idiotic whim.

THOMAS DIXON, JR., MINISTER/CINEMATOGRAPHER

Women will dress for health instead of for show—trusting their healthy faces to do all the necessary "keeping up appearances."

JOHN HABBERTON, EDITOR/AUTHOR

The dress of woman will be simpler, and the conduct of man will be more honorable—for each 100 years makes woman and man less of a fool.

DAVID SWING, THEOLOGIAN

It is a somewhat remarkable fact that human nature has never changed. In a century, man will wear a different style of garment externally, but the heart remains the same.

JOSEPH HOWARD, JR., JOURNALIST

What is the future of temperance legislation in the United States?

The dramshop will become extinct.

W. A. PEFFER, KANSAS POLITICIAN

The saloon is certain to be outlawed.

THOMAS DIXON, JR., MINISTER/CINEMATOGRAPHER

I think that less attention will be paid to temperance legislation in the 1990s and more to the study of the human stomach. Bad cooking, especially as we find it in poor hotels on the road, is the parent of many drunkards.

BILL NYE, HUMORIST

The world will have realized the folly of trying to legislate upon appetites. It will realize the necessity of educating drunkards—and that to educate them we must begin with parents. People who refuse to be taught on this and kindred subjects must be prevented from becoming parents. In this way only can drunkenness be lessened.

ELLA WHEELER WILCOX, POET

The American people will have become educated to such an extent that the vice of intemperance will largely cease. Saloons or public drinking places will no longer exist.

SIDNEY G. BROCK, POLITICIAN/AUTHOR

Temperance legislation will not only be a dead issue, but so long buried that no one will be able to identify its grave. Proper cooking and improved physical habits will have neutralized the desire for stimulants.

JOHN HABBERTON, EDITOR/AUTHOR

I am satisfied that we will have a solution to the mighty problem of temperance. This will come neither in legislative enactments nor in criminal procedure. Rather, I think that temperance is to be gained solely by the influence of the Christian religion.

DAVID H. GREER, EPISCOPAL BISHOP

What will be the state of the postal service in the 1990s?

The citizens who live in the next century are not going to pay two cents for a letter postage stamp. The price will be reduced to one cent.

THOMAS L. JAMES, U.S. POSTMASTER GENERAL

Transcontinental mails will be forwarded by means of pneumatic tubes.

FELIX L. OSWALD, NATURALIST

It is going to be possible perhaps for every citizen of the United States to have his mail delivered by free carrier at his door.

THOMAS L. JAMES, U.S. POSTMASTER GENERAL

One hundred years from now, the country will be divided into postal districts, and routine matters by the thousand will be attended to much more promptly from nearby postal centers. The United States postal service will be the greatest business machine and the most businesslike great business machine in the world.

JOHN WANAMAKER, POSTMASTER GENERAL

It will be possible for the merchants of the Mississippi Valley to send a letter to their correspondents on the Atlantic Coast in the morning and receive an answer in time for business purposes on the following day—and possibly on the same day.

THOMAS L. JAMES, U.S. POSTMASTER GENERAL

There will be electrical postal lines, carrying mail matter across the continent at a speed of 200 or 300 miles an hour. Morning newspapers in all the large cities will be delivered at the breakfast tables of their readers by this means, within a radius of 500 miles of the office of publication.

WALTER WELLMAN, ADVENTURER/JOURNALIST

It is going to be possible for businessmen in New York City and Philadelphia to communicate with each other by mail as easily during business hours as the merchants of each city can with one another now.

THOMAS L. JAMES, U.S. POSTMASTER GENERAL

What will be the state of transportation in the 1990s?

I do not believe that Robert Fulton's invention of the paddle wheel will ever be improved on for inland navigation. I am inclined to think that it may be possible, to go from New York to Chicago—and perhaps from New York to New Orleans—on inland waterways by steamboat.

ALFRED VAN SANTVOORD, SHIPPING EXECUTIVE

Lines of traffic will be straightened and highways improved, speed increased, and safety accrued.

W. A. PEFFER, KANSAS POLITICIAN

We will travel over land and water

and through the air by means of electricity.

MARY E. LEASE, REFORMER

We will hold communication with the inhabitants of other planets, and Sunday excursions to the mountains of the moon will not excite comment.

MARY E. LEASE, REFORMER

Airships will facilitate travel, and the pneumatic tube will be the means of transporting goods.

ELLA WHEELER WILCOX, POET

The problem of aerial investigation will be solved within the next 20 years. [The Wright Brothers' first flight was only 10 years away.]

FELIX L. OSWALD, NATURALIST

Man, having conquered the earth and the sea, will complete his domination over nature by the subjugation of the atmosphere. This will be the crowning triumph of the coming century. Long before the 1990s, the journey from New York City to San Francisco, across the continent—and from New York City to London, across the sea—will be made between the sunrise and sunset of a summer day.

JOHN J. INGALLS, KANSAS POLITICIAN

Men will navigate the air, and smoke will be suppressed.

W. A. PEFFER, KANSAS POLITICIAN

Considerable traveling will be done by the air route in the next century. The fact that air is an ocean which will float a man settles the question of aerial navigation. Man has simply to invent the kind of boat. It must be very large and strong. It must come.

This boat may be guided from city to city by a wire strung about 100 feet above the ground, so as to let the balloon pass over trees and houses. Thus a wire one-quarter of an inch in diameter will hold and guide many balloons full of people.

DAVID SWING, THEOLOGIAN

───────────

The railway and the steamship will be as obsolete as the stagecoach. It will be as common for the citizen to call for his dirigible balloon as it now is for him to call for his buggy or his boots.

JOHN J. INGALLS, KANSAS POLITICIAN

───────────

Aerial navigation will come within the next century. It will be accomplished not by balloons, but by the aeroplane. That aeroplane will work with stored electrical energy, operating through engines of marvelous power and lightness.

WALTER WELLMAN, ADVENTURER/JOURNALIST

There will be built a railway reaching so far that it may be possible to enter a palace car in New York City and ride it to Lima, Santiago, Rio de Janeiro, or Buenos Aires. Railroad development will do for South America what it has done for the United States.

WILLIAM R. GRACE, CAPITALIST

There will be a railway between Buenos Aires and Chicago. And the theory of Columbus concerning a western passage to the Indies will be realized by the construction of an isthmian canal.

WILLIAM ELEROY CURTIS, PAN-AMERICANIST

I presume that a speed of from 90 to 100 miles an hour could be secured with modern locomotives and with the improvements which are sure to come by the 1990s.

GEORGE WESTINGHOUSE, INVENTOR/CAPITALIST

One hundred years from now, the people of the United States will be traveling at a rate of 100 miles an hour—on electrical railways.

CHARLES FOSTER, SECRETARY OF THE TREASURY

It will be a common thing to travel from New York to Chicago in 7 or 8 hours on the train.

CHARLES FOSTER, SECRETARY OF THE TREASURY

I have no doubt at all that there will be a number of trains whose schedule time will call for as much as 100 miles an hour. I have no doubt that a traveler will be able to get his breakfast in New York City and his evening dinner in Chicago.

W. WALTER WEBB, RAILROAD EXECUTIVE

Railways will be so leveled and straightened that slow freight trains will make 100 miles an hour. The best of passenger trains will run 130 miles an hour. It is not certain that steam will be the form of power. New powers are liable to be discovered. One cent per mile will be full fare.

DAVID SWING, THEOLOGIAN

The electrical railway will carry its travelers at a much higher speed than 100 miles per hour. Then the principal trunk lines will run trains at 150 or more miles an hour. Not only will these lines elevate the tracks to secure clear way, but they also will enclose them with light structures of glass or other material to escape atmospheric impediment.

WALTER WELLMAN, ADVENTURER/JOURNALIST

There is no doubt that electricity as a motive power for passenger traffic will be extensively used in the next century.

GEORGE WESTINGHOUSE, INVENTOR/CAPITALIST

Man will perfect the system of electricity, making that power cheap and common. We shall have electric carriages, wagons, delivery carts, and bicycles.

WALTER WELLMAN, ADVENTURER/JOURNALIST

Given cheap electricity, we may expect great changes in rapid transit, household conveniences, electrical carriages to take the place of horses, elevators in business and private houses, and all sorts of machinery.

CHARLES FOSTER, SECRETARY OF THE TREASURY

The most important improvement will be in metropolitan rapid transit. The solution for the rapid-transit problem will not be found, in my opinion, in underground railways. Rather, it will

be found in elevated electric railways,
enclosed with glass.

WALTER WELLMAN, ADVENTURER/JOURNALIST

It is going to be possible to go by
steamer from New York to San Francisco without making the trip through
the Straits of Magellan. The Nicaraguan
canal is as sure to be built as tides are
to ebb and flow and the seasons to
change. [Built through Panama instead, the canal was begun 11 years
later, and opened in 1914.]

WARNER MILLER, CAPITALIST/POLITICIAN

The isthmian canal is inevitable.
The effect of its construction upon the
destiny of the United States is something almost inconceivable, if the

United States controls the canal or
if United States capital does.

WARNER MILLER, CAPITALIST/POLITICIAN

On account of fast and cheap
travel, cities will become groups of
suburbs. Thus all the poor will have air,
sunshine, and light.

DAVID SWING, THEOLOGIAN

The trolley railway is going to be
one of the mightiest factors in urban
civilization. The indications now are
that it may solve some of the problems
of overcrowding which have vexed the
social economists.

JOHN J. CARTY, CORPORATE EXECUTIVE

An urban trolley system is simply
going to annihilate distance and make
the man who lives in the country, to all

intents and purposes, an inhabitant of the nearest city.

JOHN J. CARTY, CORPORATE EXECUTIVE

By the end of the Twentieth Century, transportation facilities will have so improved that the orange district of Florida will practically furnish the United States all the oranges that it requires.

SAMUEL BARTON, FINANCIER

The means of communication will become more and more perfect. Lower California and faraway Alaska will be as near to Massachusetts, New York, and Ohio in thought and sympathy as people in adjoining states or communities are to each other.

JOHN W. NOBLE, SECRETARY OF THE INTERIOR

Is it likely that the railroads and telegraphs will be owned or managed by the state?

It is absolutely certain either that the railroads and telegraphs will be owned and managed by the state or that the railroads and telegraphs will own and manage the state.

THOMAS DIXON, JR., MINISTER/CINEMATOGRAPHER

There is no likelihood that the railroads and telegraphs will ever be managed by the state. The state would no more take charge of these industries than it would other enterprises now owned and controlled by individuals—streetcar lines, manufactures, steamship lines, and farms.

SIDNEY G. BROCK, POLITICIAN/AUTHOR

The man who, in the 1990s, talks
of the government buying and operating railroads will be looked upon by
the charitably disposed as a sort of Rip
Van Winkle. The more matter-of-fact
critics will consider him an ignoramus.
The scientific observers will conclude
he is suffering from a mild form of
dementia.

MICHAEL D. HARTER, OHIO POLITICIAN

———————

Telephone instruments, located in
every house and office, will permit the
communication of business and society
to be conducted by the voice at will
from Boston to Moscow and from
Denver to Hangchow—just as readily
as now occurs between neighboring
villages.

JOHN J. INGALLS, KANSAS POLITICIAN

———————

The railroads and telegraphs will in all probability be owned by the state and managed excellently—better than they have been at any previous time.

JUNIUS HENRI BROWNE, JOURNALIST

Railroads, water courses, telegraphs, telephones, pneumatic tubes, and all other methods of transporting passengers, freight, and intelligence will be owned and operated by the government. The earnings of these agencies will swell the public treasury.

T. V. POWDERLY, POPULIST EDITOR

Government ownership of the railways and the telegraphs would be the most serious blunder that this country could make in the coming century. Government should regulate, but not own, railways and those other concerns with which the commerce and prosperity of the people are so intimately connected.

SHELBY M. CULLOM, POLITICIAN

———————

Before the next century shall end, railroads, telegraphs, and many other things now held as private spoil will be public property.

JOHN SWINTON, LABOR JOURNALIST

———————

The railroads, the channels of communication, light, water, and all public improvements will be managed by the state, in the interest of the people, and owned by the general government.

MARY E. LEASE, REFORMER

What changes in the structure and operation of the federal government will occur by the 1990s?

The government will have grown more simple, as true greatness tends always toward simplicity.

ELLA WHEELER WILCOX, POET

American government will be much simpler than now, and it will concern itself only with fewer and more important affairs.

JOHN HABBERTON, EDITOR/AUTHOR

The American government will grow more complex. All development moves away from simplicity toward complexity. Man has more organs than the oyster. Nature began with a single cell and expanded into human civilization.

IGNATIUS DONNELLY, REFORMER/AUTHOR

Politically, there will be far less money expended in electing officials, I fancy. And many of our leading politicians out of a job will be living on the island [incarcerated]—while those now on the island will have learned that the price of one vote will not maintain them for four years.

BILL NYE, HUMORIST

The next hundred years will bring a limit of the Presidential term to six years, with no reelection.

DANIEL W. VOORHEES, INDIANA POLITICIAN

The American President will be elected for 6 or 8 years. He will not be eligible for a second term. Near the close of the next century, some rare, noble woman will be elected President of the United States.

DAVID SWING, THEOLOGIAN

One hundred years from now, I look to see a considerable part of the money needed for our government raised by means of an income tax.

DANIEL W. VOORHEES, INDIANA POLITICIAN

The selection of those who represent us in the U.S. Senate, our highest legislative body, will soon be taken from the hands of state legislatures and placed in the hands of the people, where it belongs. [That change occurred ten years later.]

WILLIAM JENNINGS BRYAN, POLITICIAN

American government will be simpler, and the initiative and referendum will prevail. Lawmakers will not be the autocrats they now are, for they will truly register the will of the people. They will not dictate to them, as at present.

T. V. POWDERLY, POPULIST EDITOR

It seems to me certain that government must grow more complex, if we understand complexity to mean the multiplication of its functions.

THOMAS DIXON, JR., MINISTER/CINEMATOGRAPHER

The American government will become more simple—both in methods of election and in its executive branch.

HEMPSTEAD WASHBURNE, POLITICIAN

Before the next century shall end, the functions and powers of our government will be greatly enlarged.

JOHN SWINTON, LABOR JOURNALIST

The election of the President by an electoral college—which often turns the contest on a few pivotal states and sometimes thwarts the will of the people—is destined to be replaced by a more direct method of ascertaining the popular will.

WILLIAM JENNINGS BRYAN, POLITICIAN

The commonwealth will be organized on industrial lines. Labor organizations will have disappeared, for there will be no longer a necessity for their existence. An ideal democracy will prevail.

T. V. POWDERLY, POPULIST EDITOR

———————

The President of the United States will have much less work on his hands than he has now—although the country will be twice as great and the government correspondingly larger. For long before that time Presidents will cease to give personal consideration to a myriad of matters which now consume their time and their energies, such as appointments to minor posts.

ELIJAH W. HALFORD, PERSONAL SECRETARY TO
PRESIDENT BENJAMIN HARRISON

The functions of government will be less coercive and more suggestive— i.e., they will relate less to the preservation of order and more to the promotion of pleasure, progress, and the diffusion of information and thought. That government will imprison fewer felons and publish more statistics.

VAN BUREN DENSLOW, ECONOMIC ANALYST

———————

Political equality cannot exist long in the midst of great social and pecuniary inequality. Thus the next century will bring an evident and growing desire to bring the government nearer to the people.

WILLIAM JENNINGS BRYAN, POLITICIAN

———————

The White House of the future will be simply the White House of the present, enlarged. I do not believe it will ever be found desirable to separate the President's residence from his office.

ELIJAH W. HALFORD, PERSONAL SECRETARY TO PRESIDENT BENJAMIN HARRISON

The limits of our federal powers are now pretty well-defined. The people have decided against any further centralization of power in this country; they do not wish federal powers to be either circumscribed or greatly enlarged. Therefore, I believe that the government will go through another century substantially as it is at the present day.

DANIEL W. VOORHEES, INDIANA POLITICIAN

What will be the state of the arts in America in the 1990s?

America will produce the greatest authors who shall be living in the 1990s. In musical achievement, it will still be behind older countries.

ELLA WHEELER WILCOX, POET

There will not be so many books printed, but there will be more said.

ANDREW C. WHEELER (NYM CRINKLE), ART CRITIC

American literature, I hope, will be more realistic. I trust there will be less colic among poets, and less vain regret and gastritis among poetesses.

BILL NYE, HUMORIST

New York City will have a great theater—perhaps modeled after that of the great theater of France. It will be supported not by the patronage of the state, but by that of individuals of wealth.

RICHARD MANSFIELD, ACTOR/PRODUCER

———————

Chicago will be the eastern head-quarters of the theatrical world, and San Francisco the western.

OCTAVUS COHEN, ARTS CRITIC

———————

The United States in the next century will be the greatest music-loving and music-producing nation on earth.

RAFAEL JOSEFFY, PIANIST

———————

By the [1990s], the popular taste in American drama will demand much the same material that served to delight our grandparents half a century ago. In other words, Shakespeare will be on top.

OCTAVUS COHEN, ARTS CRITIC

All theaters will have revolving stages, so that there will not be more than 10 seconds' wait between acts. This will, of course, do away with the vile orchestras which now torture us.

OCTAVUS COHEN, ARTS CRITIC

Actors and singers of ordinary repute will be received into the very best society. Those of particularly great reputation will be eagerly sought after by fashion's leaders.

OCTAVUS COHEN, ARTS CRITIC

———————

Each reasonably well-to-do man (and there will be lots of them in the 1990s) will have a telephote [sic] in his residence. By means of this device, the entertainment at any place of amusement in that city may be seen as well as heard. Thus there will be fewer better-class theaters than there are today.

OCTAVUS COHEN, ARTS CRITIC

———————

The 1990s will bring us the sound book in some form, and with that the intellectual equipoise of mankind will begin to be restored.

JOHN CLARK RIDPATH, AUTHOR

The principal change which will occur in American literature will be that there will be an American literature.

VAN BUREN DENSLOW, ECONOMIC ANALYST

By the agency of forces just beginning to be understood, it is possible that the reporter and the editor will no longer be compelled to write. Rather, the spoken word may appear immediately imprisoned in cold type.

E. J. EDWARDS, NEWSPAPER COLUMNIST

I do not see how anyone can diligently investigate the current examples of American literature without perceiving that its slow advance is toward a better humanity, a closer fraternity, a broader charity. These signs are unmistakable.

ANDREW C. WHEELER (NYM CRINKLE), ART CRITIC

In a century, without doubt, there will be established a purely American literature, one as distinctive as that of any other old country of today. Music and drama will follow the literature of the day.

HEMPSTEAD WASHBURNE, POLITICIAN

In the Twentieth Century, Americans will create a distinctly American drama. It will be as artistic, as perfect, and of as great an influence as that which has characterized the national drama of France.

A. M. PALMER, THEATRICAL EXECUTIVE

What changes do you foresee in the development of the South and of the West?

Before the next Columbian centennial, the South will be the empire manufacturing region of the continent.

HENRY V. BOYNTON, JOURNALIST

The Piedmont region of the South will, long before the next Columbian centennial, be the New England of the new South. This is the region of the Appalachian ranges and their foothills, from the Potomac River to central Georgia and Alabama.

HENRY V. BOYNTON, JOURNALIST

The most stupendous changes in

the United States during the next 100 years are to come in the Far West. All through that region—much of which is now arid and not populated—will be a population as dense as the Aztecs ever had in their palmiest days in Mexico and Central America. Irrigation is the magic wand which is to bring about these great changes.

JOHN W. NOBLE, SECRETARY OF THE INTERIOR

———————

The whole vast West will be irrigated and fertilized, furnishing food for all our population.

ELLA WHEELER WILCOX, POET

———————

Forest reservations will comprise the upper ridges of all our Eastern American mountain ranges, and large areas of the arid West will be redeemed by a multitude of orchard farms.

FELIX L. OSWALD, NATURALIST

The development of the great West, and especially of the South and the Southwest will, I think, be as prodigious as has been that of the states of the Ohio Valley under the influence of railway construction.

WILLIAM R. GRACE, CAPITALIST

Will there be any changes in the state of the American monetary system by the 1990s?

Concerning the future of our monetary system: the remedy is an international paper money that all the wealth of the world would back up and sustain legal tender among all nations. This paper money would be increased in precise ratio to the increase in population or in the wealth of the world.

IGNATIUS DONNELLY, REFORMER/AUTHOR

Probably the government will own and control all the products of our gold and silver mines. These products will be held by the government, as now, for the purpose of redeeming the paper obligations of the government. However, such redemption will largely be unnecessary—for the reason that there will be such stability in our financial laws that the people will not question the value of any of the obligations of the government.

SIDNEY G. BROCK, POLITICIAN/AUTHOR

Money changers will be shorn of their power. There will be no usury nor mortgages—the year of jubilee will have come!

W. A. PEFFER, KANSAS POLITICIAN

What developments do you foresee in the legal profession by the 1990s?

Law will be simplified and brought within the range of the common people. As a result, the occupation of two-thirds of the lawyers will be destroyed. At present, law is a stupendous swindle.

THOMAS DIXON, JR., MINISTER/CINEMATOGRAPHER

Pretty generally across the nation, lawyers will become specialists. I suspect that what we now know as an all-around lawyer then will be a very rara avis.

ABRAM DITTENHOEFER, ATTORNEY

Law will be simplified in the United States. Lawyers will have diminished in number, and their fees will have been vastly curtailed.

JUNIUS HENRI BROWNE, JOURNALIST

———————

Almost every community or town will be within speaking distance of the greater cities. Distances will be obliterated. This facility of communication will take those who have legal business to the cities. For that reason, there will be, in fact, no country lawyers.

ABRAM DITTENHOEFER, ATTORNEY

What will be the state of U.S. divorce laws in the 1990s?

All marriages will be happy—for the law will put to death any man or woman who assumes conjugal position without the proper physical, mental, and financial qualifications.

JOHN HABBERTON, EDITOR/AUTHOR

In the American future, a marriage entered into without intellectual and moral affinities will be condemned, as prostitution is now.

ANNIE BESANT, REFORMER

I should expect to see the divorce laws of the country much more harmonious than they are at the present time.

But I believe our divorce laws will continue to be the enactment of states and not of the federal Congress.

WILLIAM H. H. MILLER, U.S. ATTORNEY GENERAL

Marriage will be not so much a contract of flesh, legalized for a fee, as a union of soul sanctified by an approving conscience.

MARY E. LEASE, REFORMER

The divorce laws will be the same in all the states. Divorce will be freer generally than at present. But it will be allowed for only a few moral causes—among them non-support, disloyalty, crime, intemperance, and temperamental incompatibility.

JUNIUS HENRI BROWNE, JOURNALIST

Will our soil and methods of agriculture improve so as to provide food without difficulty for all of our population in the 1990s?

Agriculture will be developed by electricity. Science will take, in condensed form from the rich loam of earth, the life force or germs now found in the heart of the corn, in the kernel of the wheat, and in the luscious juice of the fruits. A small phial of this life from the fertile bosom of Mother Earth will furnish man with subsistence for days. And thus the problems of cooks and cooking will be solved.

MARY E. LEASE, REFORMER

The contents of sewers will not flow into our rivers and streams, to send deadly vapors into the air. Rather they will be utilized to enrich the harvest-yielding earth.

T. V. POWDERLY, POPULIST EDITOR

The slaughter of animals—the appetite for flesh meat that has left the world reeking with blood and bestialized humanity—will be one of the shuddering horrors of the past. Slaughter houses, butcher shops, and cattle pens will be converted into conservatories and beds of bloom.

MARY E. LEASE, REFORMER

The American farmer must either find new wheat lands by a well-considered and elaborate general system of irrigation or special methods of cultivation. Or else the American people will be compelled in the next century to import instead of export wheat.

WILLIAM R. GRACE, CAPITALIST

On the 500th Columbian anniversary, the population of America will be enormous. Consequently all soil worth tilling will receive the best possible attention—with the result that we will be the best fed nation in the world.

JOHN HABBERTON, EDITOR/AUTHOR

New and simpler forms of electric railways will enable all populous rural regions to enjoy the benefits of rapid transit and cheaper transportation. Individual farmers will have their own lines for the movement of products to the main line.

WALTER WELLMAN, ADVENTURER/JOURNALIST

American genius is going to show Europe how nutritive and desirable American corn is for food purposes when it is properly cooked.

WILLIAM R. GRACE, CAPITALIST

Methods of agriculture will be such, and the improvement in agricultural machinery so great, that all the immense population of the 1990s will be amply provided for. American citizens will continue to be the best dressed, the best fed, and the best housed people of the world.

SIDNEY G. BROCK, POLITICIAN/AUTHOR

What will be the status of women—particularly regarding suffrage—in the 1990s?

It will be possible for women to walk from house to house, in city or country, in safety; girls may go to church or to school, or even take a harmless walk in the fields or woods, without danger of being waylaid and murdered by their "natural protectors."

ELIZABETH AKERS ALLEN, POET

It is not improbable that women may obtain the right of franchise in many states by the 1990s. Her social status will then, as now, be what she herself makes it.

HEMPSTEAD WASHBURNE, POLITICIAN

Woman will be financially independent of man, and this will materially lessen crime. No longer obliged to rifle her husband's pockets for money, she will not give birth to kleptomaniacs or thieves.

ELLA WHEELER WILCOX, POET

Woman shall have the sole right to say when she shall wear the crown of motherhood.

MARY E. LEASE, REFORMER

Women will never want the right of suffrage—that is, there will not be enough of them that want it to even encourage the menfolks to give it to them.

BILL NYE, HUMORIST

We have reasonable ground for believing that women will share with men all the duties of citizenship.

W. A. PEFFER, KANSAS POLITICIAN

In the American society of the 1990s, the sexes will co-operate for mutual service. Each will bring its special powers to the help of the race, without artificial restrictions on either.

ANNIE BESANT, REFORMER

Women will never largely control the coercive or military functions of government.

VAN BUREN DENSLOW, ECONOMIC ANALYST

Woman, having more leisure in the next century, will elevate her

political and social status from subordi-
nation to equality with men.

JOHN J. INGALLS, KANSAS POLITICIAN

Woman will have equal rights
with man. She will be free to select a
husband, instead of waiting for a man
to ask her hand.

JOHN HABBERTON, EDITOR/AUTHOR

Woman will attain her status of
equality before the law.

THOMAS DIXON, JR., MINISTER/CINEMATOGRAPHER

The social and political status of
women will be on a par with that of
men. They will enjoy the elective
franchise.

JUNIUS HENRI BROWNE, JOURNALIST

What developments will most affect the American Indian in the Twentieth Century?

The number of Indians at the present time is about 250,000. A hundred years hence, they will number one million or so [1990 census: 1,959,000]. This increase will be due to the cessation of wars, the spread of intelligence and morality, the improvement of hygienic conditions, the disappearance of the medicine man, the better food supply, and the intermarriage with whites.

The Indian tribes will disappear by the end of the next century, and agencies will become a thing of the past—thus disposing of the much-abused Indian agents, whether civilians or Army officers.

Thomas J. Morgan,
Commissioner of Indian Affairs

The great body of Indians will become merged in the indistinguishable mass of our population. And there will spring up a new aristocracy, claiming distinction by reason of Indian descent. To be able to trace one's pedigree back to some great warrior or big chief, or to have the right to claim descent from one of the first graduates of Carlisle, will be almost as desirable as to belong to New York's "Four Hundred."

Thomas J. Morgan,
Commissioner of Indian Affairs

Many Indians will achieve distinction as orators, poets, financiers, and inventors. Some of the finest poetry ever penned will find its inspiration and material in Indian history. And a whole generation of novelists will win fame and favor by stories whose leading characters are of Indian descent. An Indian will command the United States Army.

THOMAS J. MORGAN,
COMMISSIONER OF INDIAN AFFAIRS

Some Indian tribes will become wholly extinct, leaving scarcely a trace of their history outside of the records of the Indian Bureau.

THOMAS J. MORGAN,
COMMISSIONER OF INDIAN AFFAIRS

What developments will occur in architecture by the 1990s?

Architects will go on making pretty drawings of dwelling houses, which will not have any closets, and the hall will contain the woodbox and the lavatory, as it does now.

BILL NYE, HUMORIST

The world will shine with the new luster of its principal metal, aluminum. All things shall become whiter than silver. All the exterior aspects of life shall be burnished to brightness. The houses and the cities of men, built of aluminum, shall flash in the rising sun with surpassing brilliance.

JOHN CLARK RIDPATH, AUTHOR

Millions of dwelling houses will be

artificially cooled in summer, as they are now heated in winter.

FELIX L. OSWALD, NATURALIST

The finest churches, the most beautiful architecture, the most exquisite parks, the most magnificent drives will give comfort and delight to the people who live in this community in the next century. There are to be reforms of municipal administration.

ANDREW H. GREEN, NEW YORK CITY ADMINISTRATOR

All the forests in the United States will be gone. Lumber will be so scarce that stone, iron, brick, slag, etc. will be largely used in the construction of houses. As a result, fires will be almost unheard of, and insurance companies will go out of business.

JOHN HABBERTON, EDITOR/AUTHOR

What improvements, inventions, and discoveries in mechanics and industrial arts do you foresee by the 1990s?

It is as useless to attempt to foretell the century-hence improvements in mechanics, in industrial arts, and in modes of travel as it would have been 40 years ago for any one to have anticipated the telephone and its now-universal use.

HEMPSTEAD WASHBURNE, POLITICIAN

The next 100 years will develop changes more stupendous than have been shown by the last 100 years—in which pretty nearly every useful thing there is in the world has been invented.

CHARLES FOSTER, SECRETARY OF THE TREASURY

It is entirely possible (nay, quite probable) that we will have a method of storing energy so it can be shipped in small packages and applied wherever wanted. Then every little town—every rural neighborhood, perhaps—can have its own little cotton or woolen mill. And the farmer can plow his fields and heat his dwelling with a storage battery no bigger than a common brick.

J. H. BEADLE, JOURNALIST

Domestic life and avocations will be rendered easier, less costly, and less complex by the distribution of light,

heat, and energy through storage cells
or from central electric stations.

JOHN J. INGALLS, KANSAS POLITICIAN

———————

The probable developments in
electricity in the Twentieth Century are
almost inconceivable. I am inclined to
think that, not many years hence,
electricity will be found serving the
household exactly as gas, steam, and
coal now serve it—for cooking, heating, and lighting purposes.

JOHN J. CARTY, CORPORATE EXECUTIVE

———————

Thomas Edison will find the pump
that will extract electricity or terrestrial
magnetism (or whatever it is) from the
earth at a cost so low (one-tenth the
present rate) as to make electricity the
universal power.

CHARLES FOSTER, SECRETARY OF THE TREASURY

Motion will supply light, heat, and power, and there will be no waste of fuel.

W. A. PEFFER, KANSAS POLITICIAN

The chief discoveries of the late Twentieth Century will consist in producing fire out of water, silver out of clay, strong and permanent buildings out of paper, a locomotive force out of gravity, diamonds out of charcoal— and in making it always possible (because profitable) for every intelligent person to travel.

VAN BUREN DENSLOW, ECONOMIC ANALYST

Inventions and discoveries in mechanics and industrial arts will themselves form, in their enlargement, the basis of the new society which will be evolved in the new century. Pneumatic transportation as well as aerial navigation seems to be certain within the next 25 years.

THOMAS DIXON, JR., MINISTER/CINEMATOGRAPHER

The kitchen stove will give place to ranges heated by water-gas, and men and children (as well as women) will know how to cook. People of means will eat to live—not live to eat.

JOHN HABBERTON, EDITOR/AUTHOR

There will be no delivery of coal at the houses, as is now the case. Coal will be taken to a central station and there converted into electric energy, exactly as is the case now in the manufacture of gas. This central agency will furnish the electric current for heating, lighting, and cooking purposes in many houses. The economy will be very great.

JOHN J. CARTY, CORPORATE EXECUTIVE

Electricity itself may be the great destructive agent employed in military operations in the Twentieth Century.

JOHN J. CARTY, CORPORATE EXECUTIVE

Among the greatest changes that the 1990s will discover will be the substitution of aluminum for iron, and that of sound for sight in the work of learning. Both of these substitutions imply a striking change in the relations of man to the laws of his environment.

JOHN CLARK RIDPATH, AUTHOR

By harnessing the power of Niagara Falls in the next century, we can supply all local manufacturers, as well as furnish the city of Buffalo with light and with electricity for domestic uses. In fact, this source may even provide power and light for cities as far away as New York and Philadelphia on the east and Cleveland, Cincinnati, and Toledo on the west.

ALBERT D. SHAW, DIPLOMAT/EXECUTIVE

Improvements, inventions, and startling discoveries will so crowd and supersede one another in the next century that our limited human ken cannot today grasp them all.

MARY E. LEASE, REFORMER

I cannot rid myself of the belief that we are on the eve of an industrial

revolution as a result of electrical re-
search and experiment. It will be the
destiny of the American people to lead
the nations on to a more perfect—and
as yet undreamed of—civilization.

CHARLES FOSTER, SECRETARY OF THE TREASURY

Electricity will be the motive power
of the future.

MARY E. LEASE, REFORMER

Where will be the greatest city in America in the 1990s?

Chicago! It is a vortex, with a constantly increasing circumference, into which the wealth and population of the richest and most fertile area of the earth's surface is constantly concentrating. By the 1990s Chicago will be not only the greatest city in the United States, but also in the world.

JOHN J. INGALLS, KANSAS POLITICIAN

The Mississippi Valley could revolve completely around Chicago—the largest city in the valley, with as many as 10,000,000 people. It might extend itself from Wisconsin to Indiana.

JOHN MCGOVERN, CHICAGO-BASED JOURNALIST

In all probability, Chicago. There will be wonderful cities in the West, none more beautiful and extensive than Salt Lake City. But unless all signs fail, Chicago will take precedence.

KATE FIELD, JOURNALIST/CRUSADER

Since the center of American population has moved westward 500 miles in the past century, I conclude that the greatest city in the United States in the 1990s will be located on our boundless Western prairies.

MARY E. LEASE, REFORMER

One of the greatest cities in the United States will be found to occupy the area between Buffalo and Niagara Falls. There will be a city of one million inhabitants there. It will be one of the

greatest manufacturing cities in the
world.

ALBERT D. SHAW, DIPLOMAT/EXECUTIVE

The greatest city in America and
the greatest city in the world in the
Twentieth Century will be that com-
prised in the metropolitan district of
New York. The New York of the 1990s
will have more than 8,000,000 people
[1890 New York population was 1.5
million; in 1990, 7.3 million].

ANDREW H. GREEN, NEW YORK CITY ADMINISTRATOR

Denver will be as big as New York
and in the center of a vast population.

ANDREW C. WHEELER (NYM CRINKLE), ART CRITIC

I think that our pleasure-seekers will discover that the lower part of Florida has as many temptations in the winter season as have any of the winter resorts of Europe. I look to see the islands of the Caribbean sea become the resort of those who seek fashionable pleasures.

SAMUEL BARTON, FINANCIER

It is not improbable that some industrial emporium of the "Piedmont country"—perhaps Birmingham, Alabama—will become the great American city of the future.

FELIX L. OSWALD, NATURALIST

We are going to have great cities, such as have not been. Their whereabouts I do not know—but all the world is going to town! Machinery has emancipated man from the fields.

JOAQUIN MILLER, POET/AUTHOR

Cities will become great only as workshops.

VAN BUREN DENSLOW, ECONOMIC ANALYST

As for cities, we will build new ones, on pleasant, beautiful sites, as men now build hotels. Even now millions are waiting for those who will build a new city—complete with sewers, pipes, pavements, all things—and empty the unclean and rotten old into the healthful and pleasant new.

JOAQUIN MILLER, POET/AUTHOR

In the next century, the value of Florida to the United States will be of more commercial importance than are some of those Western states in which bonanza mines have been discovered.

There will be a wonderful development of Florida. Our people do not understand what a magnificent territory that is. It will become not only the great sanitarium for the invalids of the East, but it also will be a rival with Nice and other Mediterranean districts for those who seek pleasure and comfort in winter travel.

SAMUEL BARTON, FINANCIER

What American (now living) will be the most honored in the 1990s?

If any man now living solves the great question of the true relationship of capital and labor, to him will the 1990s accord the honor of the greatest man. Next to him stands Thomas Edison.

ELLA WHEELER WILCOX, POET

The best remembered American in the 1990s? Why, Edison, of course.

JOAQUIN MILLER, POET/AUTHOR

Grover Cleveland, if he fulfills the expectations of his best friends....the George Washington and Abraham Lincoln of this generation.

KATE FIELD, JOURNALIST/CRUSADER

I hope that the most honored American in the 1990s will be George Washington.

GEORGE ALFRED TOWNSEND, JOURNALIST/AUTHOR

———————

Washington and Lincoln will still be the most honored names—because no other two minds can again find two such tasks to be performed.

DAVID SWING, THEOLOGIAN

That man who is most abused by the men of his generation—and yet who lives the truth in the noblest and truest ways.

THOMAS DIXON, JR., MINISTER/CINEMATOGRAPHER

———————

I am offering odds that it will not be the son of a wealthy man, but some poor boy at present with chapped wrists and chilblains on his heels, whose heart is full of hope and whose terror now is soap.

BILL NYE, HUMORIST

The most honored American now living will probably be [agnostic lecturer] Robert G. Ingersoll. For deep odium while one lives is the surest test of a man being far enough in advance of his time to be hated by his contemporaries and, therefore, revered by posterity....If Ingersoll shall be most honored by the multitude in the 1990s, it will not prevent Thomas A. Edison from being most honored by the scientific class.

VAN BUREN DENSLOW, ECONOMIC ANALYST

Will the race be happier, healthier, and handsomer in the 1990s than it is now?

At the Quincentennial, 300 million Americans will celebrate the landing of Columbus [1990 census: 248 million]. They will be educated and refined, for the arts and sciences will be taught in the public schools.

T. V. POWDERLY, POPULIST EDITOR

Long before the 1990s, America will have no very rich or very poor. And the family will be restricted to the capacity of the parents to maintain and educate it.

T. V. POWDERLY, POPULIST EDITOR

If our men keep pace with our women in athletic development and in clean morals through the Twentieth Century, the race will be larger and handsomer. Otherwise we shall produce splendid amazons and pygmy men.

ELLA WHEELER WILCOX, POET

American society in the 1990s will comprise the most perfect civilization and the most prosperous and happy people that the world ever knew.

ASA C. MATTHEWS, FINANCIER

Longevity will so increase that lives of 120 years will be as frequent as now are those of 90.

VAN BUREN DENSLOW, ECONOMIC ANALYST

Whether the race proves to be happier, healthier, and handsomer all depends on our women. If they marry for love and not for convenience, if they cultivate the inside of their heads as sedulously as they now study fashion, and if they teach their children self-respect and respect for authority, then the race will improve.

KATE FIELD, JOURNALIST/CRUSADER

———————

In 100 years Americans will have more leisure to think. The present rate of headlong material activity cannot be kept up for another century.

ANDREW C. WHEELER (NYM CRINKLE), ART CRITIC

———————

All Americans will have happy homes. Vice and immorality will have largely, if not altogether, ceased to exist. There will be not only great intellectual advancement, but also very great moral advancement.

SIDNEY G. BROCK, POLITICIAN/AUTHOR

Books and music, athletic games, and mental and physical culture will occupy the time and thoughts of a healthy, happy, godlike people—who will send out thought messages from soul to soul, from place to place, as an arrow flies from the bow of the archer.

MARY E. LEASE, REFORMER

In the Twentieth Century, great calamities will come to America in the form of pestilence, earthquakes, and civil strife, but they will not impede the general progress of the nation.

DAVID SWING, THEOLOGIAN

The race doubtless will be handsomer, and it will be more refined in its general makeup and manners. Perhaps the race will be not so healthy, though, for it will drift more toward sedentary habits. And perhaps it will not be any happier, because of the greater struggle then for existence, caused by the greater population and increased competition.

HEMPSTEAD WASHBURNE, POLITICIAN

The whole tendency of the race will be toward comfort, leisure, luxury, cultivation, simplicity in dress, and broader charity in all social relations. The race will be handsomer, healthier, and happier than ever before in the history of the world.

SIDNEY G. BROCK, POLITICIAN/AUTHOR

The progress of the lower grades of animal life has been skillfully guided and hastened, until we may now assert that cattle and fowl are approaching perfection. In the 1990s the same attention will be bestowed on the human race. Instead of rushing blindly forward, increasing and multiplying at haphazard, humanity will knowingly and intelligently advance to higher altitudes.

T. V. POWDERLY, POPULIST EDITOR

There is no apparent limit—except the limit of the world itself—to the growth of wealth, to the augmentation of opportunity, and to the achievements of this American people.

ERASTUS WIMAN, CORPORATE EXECUTIVE

The United States in the 1990s

By the 1990s, if the republic remains politically compact and does not fall apart at the Mississippi River, Canada will be either a part of it or an independent sovereignty. And the northern shore of the Gulf of Mexico will be the Riviera of the western continent.

ANDREW C. WHEELER (NYM CRINKLE), ART CRITIC

———————

Europe is influencing us greatly, and that will last long and probably will be for our good. What could we learn from North Carolina or Indiana that would be better than what we could gain from European intercourse?

GEORGE ALFRED TOWNSEND, JOURNALIST/AUTHOR

———————

Even in the distant 1990s, there can never be more than the two great political parties in this country.

CHAUNCEY M. DEPEW, U.S. SENATOR

I have no fear that America will grow too big. This republic is not going to get so large that it will fall to pieces of its own weight. Nor will the people widely separated by distance suffer from a lack of heterogeneousness or common sympathy.

JOHN W. NOBLE, SECRETARY OF THE INTERIOR

While the risk of a religious war has been greatly overrated, the danger of a war of races has been quite as much underrated. The progress of education is gradually assimilating the intelligent classes of all creeds—but race instincts are less transient than dogmas, and the negro problem will yet loom up as the black specter of the North American continent.

FELIX L. OSWALD, NATURALIST

The commercial development of the United States in the Twentieth Century will be prodigious. While we are destined to be the greatest agricultural nation in the world, we are also just as surely reaching forward for commercial and manufacturing supremacy.

MATTHEW C. D. BORDEN, COTTON EXECUTIVE

I believe that we in the United States will have the most perfect republican form of government that was ever conceived in the minds of the wisest statesmen. The social condition of the people will be such that there will be no suffering from the deprivation of the necessities of life.

SIDNEY G. BROCK, POLITICIAN/AUTHOR

The idea of government will have disappeared. The people will tolerate nothing more than an entity that administers, on business principles, programs too great or too complex for private management.

JOHN HABBERTON, EDITOR/AUTHOR

I think that the growth of America will be toward simplicity. By then the American people will learn the important lesson that simple and honest living is the goal to which men should bend their energies.

EDGAR W. HOWE, JOURNALIST

Great corporations and business combines, which constitute the power of plutocracy, shall be controlled and dominated by nationalism—the creature shall not be greater than its creator.

MARY E. LEASE, REFORMER

The social and political condition of the country will be, in my opinion, a marked improvement on what it is now. It will tend more and more to humanity, reason, freedom, and independence of the individual. Socialism, which is in the air, will steadily grow here in a modified and rationalized form. There will be more equality in education, position, and fortune.

JUNIUS HENRI BROWNE, JOURNALIST

Somewhere the nation will have an intellectual capital with a national library and a national theater. It will have developed an art school of its own.

ANDREW C. WHEELER (NYM CRINKLE), ART CRITIC

The republic will be more than ever democratized. The government will be simpler.

JUNIUS HENRI BROWNE, JOURNALIST

Dry-goods dealers add departments of groceries to their general stores. They are running thousands of smaller dealers, throughout the city, out of the market. It is only a question of time until this tendency toward centralization and absorption becomes universal in all industries.

THOMAS DIXON, JR., MINISTER/CINEMATOGRAPHER

In the Twentieth Century, great corporations and business aggregations will tend toward more perfect centralization—until the monopolies become so obnoxious that they will be regulated by federal and local statutes.

HEMPSTEAD WASHBURNE, POLITICIAN

Centralization is the law of the future.

MIRIAM LESLIE, PUBLISHING EXECUTIVE

The World in the 1990s

I do not believe there will be a crowned head of the civilized world at the close of the next century.

THOMAS DIXON, JR., MINISTER/CINEMATOGRAPHER

The map of Europe will be changed. Crowns will fail and thrones will crumble. The divine right of kings and the divine right of capital will be recognized as subterfuges, whereby the vicious and the idle lived upon the toil of others. The reign of justice will be inaugurated.

MARY E. LEASE, REFORMER

In politics the people as a control-ling power are coming to the front more or less rapidly in even the oldest empires of earth. It needs no prophet to foretell that in the 1990s the world will have become equalized in every respect, even to dire monotony.

MIRIAM LESLIE, PUBLISHING EXECUTIVE

The increasing frequency of summer droughts will confront the farms of our middle states with the alternative of [facing] ruin or [initiating] forest culture. The reckless destruction of woodlands has never failed to make the summer drier and warmer and the winter floods more destructive.

FELIX L. OSWALD, NATURALIST

I think that I can see an ocean-bound republic over every part of which the Stars and Stripes will proudly wave. This would be an American republic which shall embrace not only the present United States and Alaska, but all the remainder of the North American continent now under British, Mexican, or minor domination. It will be a government of perhaps 60 states of the Union.

ASA C. MATTHEWS, FINANCIER

There will be free trade throughout the North American continent and possibly free trade with all the world.

ASA C. MATTHEWS, FINANCIER

I expect to see our present form of government substantially preserved— and extended gradually over Mexico, Canada, and British America, as well as the states of Central America.

ASA C. MATTHEWS, FINANCIER

Our federation of states will comprise Canada and probably Mexico to the Isthmus of Tehuantepec [west of the Yucatan Peninsula]. Before 1920 this isthmus will be crossed by a ship railway.

Felix L. Oswald, naturalist

Mexico and Canada will be in the North American republic and will furnish homes for many new millions.

David Swing, theologian

The manifest destiny of the United States is to dominate the American hemisphere. This will be accomplished not by political intrigue, not by diplomatic negotiations, not by the force of arms, not by the annexation of territory, and not by the establishment of protectorates—but by the influence of example and by commercial relations. The tie that will bind the American republics and colonies will be the tie of trade.

WILLIAM ELEROY CURTIS, PAN-AMERICANIST

All of North America will be under one government, managed by a council consisting of a few men. The people will own and manage all instruments of commerce, every means for supplying public needs, all sources of fuel supply, and all unused lands.

W. A. PEFFER, KANSAS POLITICIAN

By the end of the Twentieth Century, the several Latinized languages of Western Europe—English, French, German, Spanish, and Italian—

will have become quite one language, by a process of constant reciprocal borrowing of new words and because of their Saxon-Roman blending.

VAN BUREN DENSLOW, ECONOMIC ANALYST

———————

With the world open as a field, with taxation reduced to a minimum, without the need of a standing army, with an abundant supply of raw materials, and with food products cheaper than elsewhere in the world—the destiny of the United States will include the creation of an intense commerce with foreign lands.

ERASTUS WIMAN, CORPORATE EXECUTIVE

———————

If the governments in Washington and Ottawa will pass a single free-trade act, the commercial area of the United

States will be doubled—without the drawing of a sword, without the shedding of a drop of blood, and without the expenditure of a single dollar.

ERASTUS WIMAN, CORPORATE EXECUTIVE

In the next century, it will be found that American cotton manufacturers will have wrested the markets of the world from the great manufacturers of England.

MATTHEW C. D. BORDEN, COTTON EXECUTIVE

The Twentieth Century is going to be a great era for South America, and that continent cannot flourish without benefiting the United States.

WILLIAM R. GRACE, CAPITALIST

Last Words

There is the possibility that the world may be a heap of ashes or knocked to flinders by the 1990s. All geologists agree in saying that the world is already on fire inside.

THOMAS DE WITT TALMAGE, THEOLOGIAN

Go into the Patent Office and see what we have done in the last 100 years. With that before him, no man dare set a limit as to what may be done in the next 100 years.

JOHN W. NOBLE, SECRETARY OF THE INTERIOR

I cannot foretell the course or the operations of the whirligig of time. But I am disposed to surmise that the historian who in the 1990s makes record thereof will have to get up a big book.

JOHN SWINTON, LABOR JOURNALIST

Of all these forecasts, one thing may be said with tolerable certainty: Not one of them will be verified in its essential details.

J. H. BEADLE, JOURNALIST